They Tried to Break Me

They Tried to Break Me

Matthew Petchinsky

They Tried to Break Me: A True Story of Survival
By: Matthew Edward Petchinsky

"I was never the one who believed in monsters. Until I was proven, by humans, that they exist."- C.R. Bittar

Introduction

I am a child of divorce, abuse, rape and other issues. My life is full of abuse and there have been rapes on several occasions. I am here to tell you my story, I need to let all the demons come to light. I have tried to let these memories go that I am about to tell you, but it is difficult to forget. I have depression and extreme anxiety because of all the things that happened in my life that I am about to share with you. Thank you for reading this book.

-Matthew Edward Petchinsky

My life, I thought was going to be a normal good life, but fate and other things had other plans for me. The issues began when I was around 4 years old, I remember having a female teen babysitter in a plaid skirt that my parents hired to watch me. I recall her telling me she wanted to play a game. The game was where she had me completely exposed and naked, lying on the floor.

I remember her touching my little penis, and her not removing her skirt just her underwear and she got on top of me and proceeded to rape me. I was a four-year-old, how was I supposed to react to this? She took advantage of me, and no one has ever known because I at the time didn't know what was going on. I still have flashes from this event every now and then. I don't understand why anyone would rape a four-year-old child.

My parents later put me in a daycare shortly after, I remember the lady liked to be called "Mrs. Becky". I remember when I went there, she acted nice in front of the parents, but when she had the children alone, she proceeded to yell at the children. If you didn't listen to her, she would take you each individually to a separate room and spank you bare handed with your pants and underwear around your ankles. I remember her doing this to me several times.

I remember one or more times, when I didn't want to eat the cream corn or the canned peas that smelled bad to me, Mrs. Becky proceeded to try and force feed me the food, when I refused, she grabbed me by the ear and pulled my ear and dragged me down the hall throw me over her knee, pulled my pants and underwear down and began to whoop my butt bare handed.

The pain I recall was unbearable, I could hear her hand swoop through the air as she was spanking me. I recall another time while being at Mrs. Becky's daycare, one of the older children there, they were somewhere between 10 or eleven, they told me they wanted to play a game in a room when we were without our clothes. I, being the four-year-old that I was didn't know better and complied.

I remember Mrs. Becky seeing what happened and she came in running with a red face, she slapped me and the older child as well across the face, but still she just basically just "punished" us by slapping in the face and making us nap out in her living room on opposites of the room. She kept the whole incident a secret and never told my parents.

There were a few times I brought my own toys to the daycare, she even accused me of stealing a toy from her, that was exactly the one I brought. I even brought my toy T-Rex a few times and the older kids grabbed it and proceeded to pulled it on either side in front of me trying to torture me and they were laughing at me as well, as a four-year-old.

These are a few examples of where my parents never asked deeper questions on what was going on.

Now, when I became five years old, my parents had a friend of theirs that my dad knew from the military base. His name is John, I remember when I was five years old, he was going to babysit me. I saw how he looked at my mom, and how she looked at him. I had an intuitive feeling that they were doing something they were not supposed to. (I at the time didn't know that it was called intuition until I got older).

I knew that my mother was getting distant before the actual divorce happened a year later. I remember when my dad and I went fishing, we were walking back from the local pond, my mom was wearing a towel in her hair when we got back to the house. I felt something was being hidden from my dad. I at the time couldn't figure it out, but I had a feeling something was off.

I remember being sick a lot, almost every night we would rush to the emergency room, I have Hydrocephalus and there were pains with the VP shunt as I mentioned in my other book *My life with Hydrocephalus.*

I remember getting up at 2 or 3am rushing to the emergency room with shunt pains, as a five-year-old how was I supposed to handle that pain?

I am not sure the exact time frame of when the divorce happened, but I do remember my parents fighting, I think I was six years old at the time, I do remember my mom packing her things and me crying to keep her from leaving, she and my dad never really explained to me at the time that my mom had cheated on my dad and that is what led them to get a divorce. I do remember blaming myself for the divorce, for the longest time I did believe I was the cause of my Mom in Nebraska leaving.

At the time, we were in Omaha, Nebraska. For the rest of this book, I will refer to my biological mom as "Mom in Nebraska". I remember talking to a lawyer and my dad dropping me off at my Mom in Nebraska's apartment on Wilsomn Street on the weekend.

My Mom in Nebraska had moved in with my dad's work friend John, which had confirmed the feeling I had two years before then. The apartment was a two-bedroom, one bathroom apartment, it is situated on the second floor. My Mom in Nebraska, had made a friend in the apartment building two buildings down the street, she had two daughters and was a single mom at the time. My mom in Nebraska of course hired her friend's daughters to babysit me. While her and John went to work at the grocery store down the road called "No Frills" and she also worked at a place called "Nobbies parties" it is party supply store. As you can probably tell, I didn't spend much time with my Mom in Nebraska much, even if she was off from work when she had me for the weekend, it was mostly garage sales or *Goodwill*, and other local thrift stores. Yes, John and her are hoarders of thrift store goods. I'll explain more into that later.

After a few months, my dad and I began to get ready to move to Texas. I was six years old at the time. I didn't know where we were heading exactly. The only time I had ever been down to Texas was to go visit my dad's parents in Friona, Texas or my mom in Nebraska's parents in Ganado, Texas. I will explain each of them later in the book.

I remember my dad and I driving in has old rusty Branco that was a faded yellow color with blue splotches that are supposed to represent a camouflage pattern but did exactly look like that because of how faded it was. I remember how my dad's face being neutral and cold on the drive down to Texas, a couple times he got sick from *McDonald's* burgers because they didn't listen to him about no onion on the burger and we had to stop so he could get off and vomit. I remember how the Air Conditioner on the Bronco didn't work well. So, we had to roll the windows down. There were a few times that the old Branco was giving us car trouble that we had to get help from people, I had bad feelings of course when I met the people, I honestly thought something bad was going to happen. Thankfully, nothing bad happened then.

When we got down to Texas, I remember we stopped at my dad's parents' place. Their house is a rundown 1960's or 70's looking home that has three bedrooms, two bathrooms, the third bedroom is now an office for my stepgrandad, (The reason I call him my stepgrandad is because he has no blood relation to me or my dad). There is a furnace vent between the kitchen and office entry way. You must step around that vent and wear shoes in the house because of the vent.

We stayed at their house for a day or two, during that time Harley(stepgrandad) told stories about random things, I can't exactly remember what they were about, but he certainly liked to make my grandma mad, and he laughed at her when he made her mad. Francis(grandma) was born with four fingers on one hand and a baby thumb as we all call it on the other, when she points at you, she uses her middle finger to point. Both have been together for over 50 years as of the time of me writing this.

I do recall my Mom in Nebraska calling my dad's parents' house to talk to me, but I could tell than as well as now by the tone of her voice that she honestly didn't want to speak to me.

After we had spent two days in Friona, Texas. We went to San Angelo, Texas, where my dad was to be stationed at Goodfellow, Air Force Base. I can't recall what the first school I was registered at when we first moved to San Angelo. I do recall being registered in Boy Scouts; well, they called it Cub scouts first.

I remember being invited over to one of the older boy's house for a sleep over. While I was there, it was late at night, I was six years old at the time, the boy's parents were asleep, when him and two of the other older boys told me they wanted to play a game. They had me suck their penises and drink their pee as well. This went on for two years, I didn't know who to tell about this, so I tried to block this out, but again I get flashes of this.

Now, back to when I was six years old. My dad began dating, unbeknownst to me, he wasn't very upfront about that. I only found out when he brought this lady named Safiye over. At first, I thought she was a nice lady, I recall her bring a dinosaur over at the time, but I didn't know that she was going to be my stepmom at the time.

I met her son and her mom, Melih and Nazire, who later would be my step grandma and stepbrother. I didn't know exactly that we would all become a family at the time. I remember being babysat while my dad and Safiye went on dates.

After a few months, summer came and I had to go to my Mom in Nebraska's place for the first time since we moved to Texas, the duration of the stay would be eight weeks as the court order. Little did I know my Mom in Nebraska would try to manipulate me to be on her side.

When it came time for me to go to my Mom in Nebraska's place, at first, we would drive from San Angelo to Oklahoma, and we would switch me off from my dad's car to my Mom in Nebraska's car.

During those rides my Mom in Nebraska and her then boyfriend John was listening to Bill Engvall tapes and especially the one where he says, "What does a dorkfish love to eat?" "A corndog"

My Mom in Nebraska whose real name is Sondra and John from the time I was six started to call me "dorkfish" this was just the beginning of years' worth of bullying, every single year. They even hit me on the back of my head even though I have a shunt in my head, they were bullying me, making my visit that I honestly didn't want to go to even worse. For a few years, I had to have summer school in Omaha, Nebraska. Around the time it was time for me to get out of the school, my Mom in Nebraska asked her friend's daughter to pick me up, but she forgot, so I went walking home, but I didn't have a key to get into the apartment, I recall my Mom in Nebraska's friend's daughter come running into the apartment building panicking, she also had a blonde friend with her. They saw me sitting by my Mom in Nebraska's apartment.

She told me not to tell my Mom in Nebraska that she forgot to pick me up. We went back to her mom's apartment.

I remember another time when my Mom in Nebraska's friend's daughter was babysitting me inside my mom in Nebraska's apartment, bullying me to where it led me to lock her out on the balcony, I can't remember how she got back inside. I remember how my Mom in Nebraska spanked me for defending myself against a bully babysitter by locking her out. I was forced to write an apology letter too. It's funny how the whole thing was twisted around to make me look like a bad person when I may have been wrong for locking her out, but she was in the wrong for bullying me to where she got off without discipline.

As for the bullying, Sondra (Mom in Nebraska), grabbed me roughly and held me in place while she turned her butt towards me and farted, when she let go and was laughing, I pushed her, I defended myself. She even let her friends bully me as well. She was never there to defend her own flesh and blood. She rather have her child bullied by her friends, than to keep her friends from bullying them. I was kicked by one of her friends named Cheryl. I used to keep a record of all the bad things Sondra had done to me in a journal, but I lost those years ago.

After summer ended it was back in the car, and back to Texas. I found out my dad had married, Safiye and she is now my stepmom, I started walking to the school that was about a mile from the house, I made a few friends with the kids in the neighborhood or so I thought at first, until one of them pushed me into a sticker patch or burr patch.

I remember having to learn Turkish to speak to my step grandma. It was difficult to learn of course. I was also taught to set the table, clean off the table, dust, clean the yard. They tried to teach me how to use a lawn mower, but I was a bit too small at six years old for that.

My Stepmom had two sheltie dogs, Laddie and Lucy, Laddie was an aggressive dog, I remember he bit me around six or seven years old. I had a bamboo stick I had found pretending to us it as a cane like *John Hammond from Jurassic Park (1993)*. Laddie saw it in my hand and must have thought I was going to hurt him with it, that he attacked and bit my left arm about an inch below my wrist. I still remember how much blood there was, there were no stitches just a band aid, it took three months for the bite to heal completely. I still have the scar as a constant reminder to this day.

I remember when I was hugging a cat and I ground my teeth together, my jaw popped out and upward on my left side of my face, I went to get help, I was in extreme pain, I went to my dad, and he said "What? What?" not getting that I was pointing at my jaw, and I felt my jaw slide back in place on its own, and when I was able to explain what had just happened, he didn't believe me and thought I was making it up. How could I make up such pain?

I remember being at my new school of *Bowie Elementary* in second grade, I had a teacher that was a bit mean to her students when it came to discipline. There was this policy that all teachers in the school, that all students had to sign their name in a composition book along with the reason why. Mrs. Banks would say in an aggressive tone "if you are going to cry, go to the bathroom and do it".

I remember having trouble understanding the works I had to do in the school, I would get bad grades 70's and lower and I would get spanked by my dad each time he got the white folder that had my class work in or my report card. He would take me into garage have me bent over in a chair and grabbed a foot long 2x4 piece of the wood and spanked me hard, he had rage at the end of each blow. He did not understand that I have a learning disability, he always thought I was "lazy", and he thought beating me with the 2x4 would get me to do better in school. I remember feeling the pain from the spankings for three days. I recently found out from a doctor here in Eagle Pass, Texas that I have a pinched nerve on my spine, located between L5 and S1, I had a CT scan done and the technicians here in Eagle Pass saw that, but why not anyone else? I have had a lot of CT scans even in my abdomen. I know that the pinch nerve came from My dad spanking with the 2x4 block of wood. He has a strong arm that you could hear the wood swing through the air and there was a 10 second break between swings, I remember this. I know he was in the wrong, spanking a child for bad grades in wrong and immoral, life doesn't care whether you get good grades or not. I remember even my step grandma bullshitting saying, "Allah is writing in his book every time you make a bad grade." Really? You think your fake God is going to give a shit about grades from school. I am not Muslim like my parents are, nor am I Christian, like the rest of my family, I am Wiccan, I follow the Egyptian Goddess Bastet. I have had to pretend to be Muslim to appease them. I never agreed with the whole philosophy of the Christian and Muslim religions.

Speaking of the school issues, I remember, when I was in eighth grade, my anxiety was so bad because of my parents being very aggressive towards me about my grades, even though I had a learning disability, I bit into my right thumb knuckle, it was deep enough to almost see nerve. I remember my knuckle was bleeding and dark purple for about three months, but it did heal after a while. My parents made my school experience a living hell; they beat me a lot if I didn't make grades that they deemed "acceptable".

Now, that I am an adult, I have learned that grades in school, didn't even matter to my future. My parents were wrong, even the college thing didn't work out for me because of my learning disability.

Oh yeah, the college thing, my parents ripped into me about that as well, they thought I was being "lazy" again, that is why to their eye is why I was not in college. We are in a new world where college is no longer the answer for a lot of people, look at my stepbrother he stopped going to college years ago, and he owns a car wrapping business.

I remember, my parent's cooking, well if you can call it cooking, when it was burned, let's start with Sondra's cooking, she only knows how to make hamburger helper and anything in a box, but she can't even bake biscuits right or a thing called "monkey bread". If you eat her food, you are in for a flavorless, burnt turd. Mostly, during those summers, I ate Pizza Rolls or Pop Tarts, no eggs or anything of the sort, because all she kept in her fridge was preservative foods, even junk foods in her pantry. Now, for my dad, when it was him and I, all he knew how to cook was tacos, but they were flavorless, or we would eat *Kid Cuisine* meals or other take out. When he met my stepmom, he got a grill, but overcooked the steaks he cooked to the point where it was nearly charcoal, even to this day he eats dry hockey puck steaks. He doesn't watch the meat, instead he rather read or play on his phone. His steaks have no flavor at all, no juiciness at all. My stepmom can barely cook herself, all she knows how to cook is Turkish meals such as dolma, or Turkish soups, it gets tiring eating those meals, even my step grandma when she was alive only cooked Turkish meals all the time. When we went to visit my dad's parents, my dad's mom, Francis did the cooking, but she burned the food, such as biscuits and burned chicken fried steak. Harley never cooked, he believes in the old ways "Women do all the cooking and cleaning."

I do recall when my dad was trying to lose weight, he put everyone in the house on the paleo diet, I was about 106 pounds when he put us all on that diet. I didn't need to lose any weight at all at that time. I have always had a weight issue. When he had everyone on the diet that wasn't working for him. I had remained 106 pounds until he decided the paleo diet wasn't working for him. The food was bland and awful tasting. It tasted like burned cinnamon on foods that had no cinnamon flavoring at all.

I learned to cook on my own and I can cook a great medium rare steak. I can cook catfish in the oven and chicken as well.

I have been forced into churches and I didn't feel comfortable in there not the Turkish Raindrop house in San Antonio. My Mom in Nebraska, since we are the subject of religion, had me got to a Christian summer camp because she made a deal with her friend to have their daughter babysit me at 15 years old. What the hell was she thinking, I was old enough to babysit my half-brother, why would I need to be babysat, when I am old enough to take care of myself?

There were times when my stepmom thought I was lying about things that she had put a hot pepper to my tongue, she even thought I was lying about how hot the pepper was, she tested it herself, and said it wasn't hot, not she had burned away her taste buds because she has been eating those for years. They proceeded to get a red-hot pepper instead of a green hot pepper to place on my tongue, I remember not being able to taste things very well for three or four days.

They kept using hot pepper on me every time they thought I was lying even when I was telling the truth, they dare not believe the truth when they themselves force you to lie for them on many, many occasions. So, who should have had pepper on their tongue again?

I remember, I believe I was 17 or 18 years old; it was just before Mother's Day. I wanted to get my step grandma a kitten that I found on *Craigslist*, I had my parents take me to get the cat since I could not drive myself. We got the cat, but shortly after we returned to my parent's home, A fight broke out between them and I. I don't recall what the fight was about, but I do remember my stepmom screaming and my dad was about to choke me, he pushed me on top of the cat that I was going to give my step grandma and screamed at me "YOU ALMOST KILLED THAT CAT!" I wasn't the one that almost killed the cat it was him for pushing on top of the poor cat. I remember feeling his grip of his hands around my neck. I don't remember how I got him to stop choking me. I do remember the cat fearing me after that because of them after that. I would not harm a cat, I love cats. I in fact bury dead cats that I find on the road sometimes, I feel bad for the poor creatures that have been hit by cars. The cats deserve a burial does not end up in a dumpster. My parents deserve to end up in a dumpster for they are toxic people that cause harm to anyone and everyone they are in contact with.

I remember when I would get sick with a kidney infection or kidney stone, or any other illnesses, they thought I was faking all of that and still waited until the last possible moment to take me to the emergency room. Even like I mentioned in my book *My life with Hydrocephalus,* my parents thought I was faking the headaches that were painful.

Regarding me getting sick, I remember when I had the kidney infection, the school called my parents to pick me up, but instead they sent a family friend instead. I was vomiting violently at their home, that they took me to the hospital. My parents weren't there when I got admitted, in fact they weren't there for three or four days, from what I remember. The family friend was there more than my own parents. I was scared then feeling alone in the hospital.

I remember being forced to drink milk, especially banana milk, I never liked milk, it upsets my stomach, but did they listen? No, they rather pressure me to drink it, I've even vomited it up in front of them, but they all thought it was an "act" and continued to pressure me to drink milk. I did get sick from it; I do remember getting sick from drinking the milk.

My stepmom would name call as well as call me "retard" she was very rude as well. I remember her telling me that I was an "embarrassment" and "talked weird". I was talking normally as far as I know. I remember her even calling my dad "retard" even her own son as well. She had anger everyday towards everyone, even her own mother. I remember her slamming doors and screaming at everyone, even to this day she does, even with her mother's passing. She is a control freak and full of OCD. If you stepped in a spot, she just mopped she will chew you out and scream at you. She doesn't like my step grandad as well, he doesn't like her, being a racist bigot himself.

Every year, if you didn't clean the house how she wanted it done or ate accidentally with the fork scrapping across your teeth she would get angry at you. She even gets bothered by people's breathing and snoring. Most of the fights my parents had were about my dad's snoring even though my stepmom snores too. My stepmom had an issue where she thought I was breathing heavily, when I was breathing normally and wasn't making any noise through my nose. She would say "stop breathing like that, breath normally." I was breathing normally, she is just mental an has issues, in fact I believe she has Misophonia.

Misophonia is a disorder where people have abnormally strong and negative reactions to ordinary sounds humans make such as chewing or breathing.

Link: Misophonia: When sounds really do make you "crazy" - Harvard Health

Misophonia: What it is, symptoms, and triggers (medicalnewstoday.com)

I have provided two links that mention what Misophonia is about.

There was never any peace in the household, there were fights every night. I learned to bottle up my anger until I blew up, I have anxiety because of my parents and depression.

My stepmom even threatened to throw her *Blackberry* cell phone at me when we were fighting, I challenged her and said, "Come on, Hit Me". That made her madder at me.

There was a time when I was trying to make brownies and she was looking over my shoulder, well more like hovering and criticizing me, I put half an inch over on the water, but I know that was okay, but she went nuts and screamed at me and I pushed her against the counter for getting in my face. She then screamed for my dad "Mark! Mark! Your son attacked me!" and my dad came to her defense and didn't listen to what I had to say. Wouldn't you act the same way if someone got in your face too?

Now, Harley my step grandad isn't innocent himself, I could tell he never liked me. I noticed that I have nothing in common with any of my family members.

When springtime came, I went to visit my Mom in Nebraska's mom. She was very rude to everyone. When she met my stepmom, she told her "You are not the child's mother".

She even tried to get me to hate my dad as well by speaking bad about him, and so did my mom in Nebraska too. I was forced to say "Yes, ma'am and Yes, sir" when I spoke to them. I know what you are thinking "Well that is manners, you needed manners". Now, wait before you go all out on that, she was the <u>ONLY ONE</u> of all my grandparents that wanted me to say that. So, isn't that a bit unusual? Harley and Francis never told me to say that only Sue and Eddie. Even when I met my stepdad's parents, they were not that way.

My Mom in Nebraska's mom, was always rude to me and she certainly showed her true colors to me around spring 2008. My step grandma who didn't speak much English was going to stay home alone while my parents took Kerim my half-brother to Disney, (I went twice, I don't like Disney, I got sick there twice and traveling is no fun with them). I told Sue that I didn't want to go visit them so I could care for my step grandma who did speak English. She quickly without missing a beat said "I hope you enjoy your life with your damn daddy" than hung up on me. The next night my mom in Nebraska called screaming at me saying "You treated my mom like shit, means you treat me like shit". I got enraged and hung up on her, she has been a problem since the beginning of my life. My Mom in Nebraska has bullied me, hit me, stole money from me, chewed me out for eating her junk food when there was no food left in the house. Let her friends bully me and her husband John Shirley. John is a Man child, if you piss him off, he runs off like a fucking toddler and doesn't talk to you for a week or two like a bitch that lost her cookie. He hit me as well, grabbed my head and forced it to look around at what he was showing me for his stupid VHS record book.

Summers were hell every year, I was either abused or left alone or made to go be babysat by people who didn't need to babysit me because I was too old for a babysitter. There was nothing fun to do, we went to the zoo, of course some of the time *Henry Dooley Zoo.*

I always contemplated running away, but how could I? I didn't know my way back to Texas, even there wasn't much better. I suffered eight weeks of the tenth level of hell every year. I was neglected and abused there. I had told those in the schools, but they didn't believe me, or their "jurisdiction" wasn't in Nebraska.

On the last year for my visit to Nebraska, I asked my Mom in Nebraska if I could push the visit back a week for a trip for Europe, but no she wasn't reasonable. She went nuts and said that I would not deprive her of a visit from me just so I could go to Europe.

Now, she still was going to get her eight weeks of course, I mean it was pointless for me to go visit her anyway, she had me confined in the house all the time like a dog to the cage and telling me not to touch her DVD player, go outside, not to call anyone on her phone unless it was her to let her know I was awake each morning. Now, by that time I had my own portable DVD player, Cell phone and it was a huge waste of time for me to go there, while everyone was getting jobs, I was behind on the job thing because of the court ordered visits that were put in place when I was six. During that entire ordeal that night about the conversation with My Mom In Nebraska, she was screaming at me over the phone throwing a fit like an over grown child that you told "no" to when they beg for a candy or toy. I remember that there was a broken metal broom that I was taking to the trash can that night, I used it to beat punching bag that my dad had in the garage, my rage went through the roof that night, I do recall cutting my hand from that broken broom stick from hitting the punching bag with it.

Oh, I forgot to mention, my Mom in Nebraska would always tell me that when I turned 13 years old that I would have to go to court in Nebraska and choose which parent I want to live with, she was trying to manipulate me to choose her.

Of course, the court thing never happened. My Mom in Nebraska is a compulsive liar. She even told me that she set her house she now owns and everything in it, is in her will to go to her friend's daughters. Now, why would you tell me this? Why have me waste my time visiting you every summer and every other Christmas, when there is no attachment?

Speaking of Christmas with her was bad as well, she would give me a gift card from her *Walmart* job to get her stuff that she wrote on a list. And there was not a peaceful Christmas. It was dule and boring just the same as the summers.

I recall when my Mom in Nebraska ran me a bath, that apparently was extremely hot to the point that my blood boiled. I couldn't feel the heat also my nerves were already damaged from being sick with strep throat a lot of times and it wasn't treated on time, because the house was like an igloo, I forgot what age I was, but when I got out, I passed out from the high boiling blood. I was out for about 45 minutes, I recall being in a blackness, I do recall seeing Bastet hovering over me telling me it wasn't my time to die yet.

When I had returned, I was laying on the floor butt naked on a towel and my Mom in Nebraska was sitting on the floor with a neutral face as if she was disappointed, I was alive. I feel she was trying to kill me and later claim it was an "accident". I do remember her trying to convince me it was my fault, but then why did she keep the house so cold in the winter?

I feel she must have tried to kill me on other occasions when I was younger, even though, I cannot remember them. The reason I say this is because of the look of disappointment on her face as if she failed again on getting rid of a cockroach that would not die.

When on the opposite side with my dad and stepmom, holidays like thanksgiving were celebrated with fights with my step grandma on why we celebrate a Christian holiday, more yelling and fighting. Christmas was celebrated in Friona, Texas. More fighting there and racism towards my Stepmom. We even fought on New Year's and was made to change our underwear and give gifts as part of the Muslim traditions.

Overall, I never had a peaceful holiday with my parents. Even now as an adult they have tried to manipulate and control me. My stepmom looked at my bank account back when I first started working at a store called *Thrift Town* and she would call me from her job at the bank where my money was and chew me out.

Vacations were no fun with my parents, there were fights with my stepmom because she thought I was "breathing weird" or because of my dad's snoring was bothering her, they had me sleep with my half-brother Kerim, he squirmed on the bed and kicked a lot in his sleep. I got sick every time we went on vacation, my parents thought I was faking being sick to get attention. We went on cruises and there was a lot of fighting and getting looks of hatred from my stepmom because she was in a bad mood and irritated with everyone. There was no peace, there was always negativity. There has never been a great experience with vacations, especially when you are being called names every day.

Even family gathering was not peaceful, I got sick during the trip to Lubbock for a family reunion, because a few days before we went there, I had been stung by a wasp, the spot where I got stung swelled up and everyone at the family reunion noticed, I even caught a fever. I was given Benadryl to help get the fever down and an ice pack, my stepmom and my dad were pissed at me, and my stepmom complained that I was "embarrassing her". She even was complaining that she is feeling like she was being judged.

At my dad's parent's 50th anniversary, I paid for my own room at the *Friona Inn*. My parents took advantage of my room and threw my dad in that room I paid for and didn't fully pay me back for that, only $40, also my dad could have slept on the pull-out couch instead of right next to me. The only reason my dad was even in my room that I paid for was because my stepmom couldn't stand is sleep apnea machine. The machine made noise that annoyed her, but with out that machine, my dad could choke in his sleep. My stepmom complained that my dad's stepdad was being racist towards her, of course that is his personality. In fact, the whole history there is rocky as well. I was told a story about my dad's stepbrother Thomas; Thomas had stolen my dad's back up keys to his car to go on a joy ride passed curfew when they were teens. When Harley had found out he blamed my dad for giving him the keys, but my dad showed him that he had his keys with him. Harley had punched Thomas his own son for doing the wrong thing, while Thomas was re-covering from that, Harley threw a $100 bill on the ground in front of him and told him to get out. Thomas was about 16 years old at the time from what I was told. What I don't understand, knowing that this happened, why would Thomas crawl back to them?

When my step grandma was alive, at her home where I moved into, she would chew me out that forks and plastic storage containers went missing. Well, she always gave those to her Turkish friends. I was the one who witnessed her death back in 2016.

I remember the night of her death; I had just made it back from work and my step grandma seemed alright after being in the hospital for two weeks. She was watching her Turkish show, and she got up to get ice, and sat back down. I went upstairs and took care of the kittens we had in the master bathroom of the master bedroom, we had to keep the kittens confined there because of our two older cats Pom Pom and Princess were aggressive towards the kittens. I was in there for ten minutes and I then went to go get my laptop to apply for the job at *Walmart*, I then heard a loud thud and rain down the stairs to see my step grandma laying underneath the TV stand that had two glass shelves with about a foot distance from top to the bottom glass shelve. I pulled her out from there and I saw her nose was broken and bleeding a lot and other parts of her face were broken. I had called the ambulance and my parents, I come to find out that my step grandma wanted my stepmom her daughter to stay with her longer, but my stepmom didn't want to, and left her alone. So, from the time they dropped her off which was around 5 or 6pm to the time of me getting home from work which was around 9:45pm to 10pm at night, she could have had the same heart attack and die just like she did in front of my eyes that day.

A few weeks after the whole incident, my stepbrother Melih moved in, he had been having relationship issues again which wasn't uncommon for him. He brought into the house, people who were doing Marijuana and other drugs as well as more negativity and alcohol in the house. Melih has a rage issue much like my stepmom, if you piss him off, he screams at you and starts throwing stuff, like he has done to one of his Ex's that lived in the house as well.

Melih also let one of his friends to live in the house as well for $600 rent, James and Melih were not good roommates, I had to deal with Melih and him partying and making noise until 3am, them making a mess in the kitchen of shot glasses and empty alcohol bottles. James left his laundry wet and in the washer for two weeks and rewashed them and left them again. He used all the towels in the bathroom per shower.

My stepmom would always call and harp about the rent that she wanted every day, but I pay it early and all bills as well. My stepmom was also kept mentioning that my step grandma left me some $1,300, but they kept forgot to give it to me after mentioning they would multiple times. Also, I had them help me with my tax return one year and they never gave me my tax return of the year 2015, I believe it was, I kept being told that they "hadn't heard anything from the tax advisor" even after a year of me asking about that, how could you not have heard about my tax return or yours? Seems kind of fishy. If you ask me. I mean I did do the tax return the first year by myself, but when they found out they were chewing me out for not asking them for help on that. So, the next year they pressured me to death to the point of annoyance and causing anger, that they wanted me to have them do my tax return. That was a mistake, in fact they know how to push my buttons and cause me to get annoyed with them.

I bet you are wandering why I had not moved out when my step grandma died. Well, I had all my savings drained for $5,000 dollars to $800 from the ex-girlfriends that took advantage of me and my stepmom requesting $1,000 dollars for my step grandma's house property taxes. I couldn't build my savings back up because when I was at *Thrift Town,* they were cutting hours, but when I started working at *Walmart* my paychecks went to bills and rent mostly, there wasn't hardly any left to save after the high bills.

There was a time that my dad drove two and a half hours from their house, shortly after my step grandma passed away, it was wintertime, there was a space heater that I was using, especially in the summer sometimes when my stepbrother left the house too cold. My dad came to get that heater for their "well" on their land, when they had a *Walmart,* 10 or 20 minutes away from their home. I used that heater because the house heater didn't work well. My dad didn't even bother to ask if I still needed that heater. My girlfriend at the time brought me a new one, I was about to get a new one, but I had trouble transporting things on the bus. My parents rather spend money on a boat, *James Avery,* Expensive other things, but when I didn't make much money and was paying all bills in the house, they rather take the heater I was using instead of spending the money on a new space heater. I had to get a lock on my door because My parents, especially my stepmom walked into my room, I caught her on the security camera I set up in the room, there was no privacy, similar to how I explained in my first book *Life on Government benefit: my family's experience.*

I later came to find out that my half-brother Kerim had become a druggy, and I already knew Kerim was an alcoholic even though he was at the time 16 years old because my parents, dad and stepmom gave him alcohol all his life since he was three years old. They tried to do the same to me, but it didn't stick entirely, I mean yes, I did drink alcohol for a little while, but I realized it was a waste to drink that and my body certainly couldn't handle it, because of my poor damaged kidney. I have been alcohol free for quite a few years. I tried that marijuana stuff, but I never liked the taste, I never got into drugs, I am the only one of my brothers that is drug free.

My parents are surprising, for people that were against drugs certainly are not getting hard of my two brothers for the drugs that take. If I were to do that, they would have had me arrested I know it. My life is better without them around my children. When I met my wife, they didn't approve of her because she has had children already, When I moved out to live with her, they tried to guilt trip me and say I am making a mistake with my life. I don't believe I made a mistake with my life; I am happy and of course for now.

I feel I was brought here to start my career as an Author like I am always meant to be, but my parents have discouraged me from doing so, especially causing me to doubt myself and destroy the originally books I wrote back in school. I am already getting back to the confidence that I must be a published writer.

There was a time back in 2019, when my girlfriend who is now my wife, when she was pregnant with our daughter, my dad and stepmom came out here to Eagle Pass, Texas to find us after I cut them off because of their toxicity, yes Mark Edward Petchinsky, Safiye Petchinsky and Kerim Edward Petchinsky came here to see if I was alive only. They are toxic people, anyone who associates with them will be back stabbed and talked about behind their backs. They are not helpful people when you ask for assistance to get out of a rut that you are in, such as being in government housing which they led you to because they were leaches off you. The Depression, Anxiety, and stress they have given me led me to go to the local *Camino Real Mental Health* facility, located here in Eagle Pass, Texas. I spent 3 days there in 2019 just before Christmas because of the level of anxiety and depression as well as my stress levels from my experience with my parents had left me. They caused mental anguish to me. No one should ever go through such abuse that it leads them to go to the mental facility, just so they could try and forget and get "better". The whole therapy and medicines don't fix the problem. They are just bandages, not an actual cure to help a person.

I advise anyone who associates with these people to include Melih Ucok, Sondra Shirley, and John Shirley avoid them like the plague, they are not your friends, the talk bad about you behind your back. They plot to use you and leave you none the wiser for it.

I know they are reading this, and they will try to deny this, but I am not lying. They even made me an outcast, a "family member" of theirs. Please family helps family not manipulate and use them like some dirty old piece of underwear then toss them to the side when finished with them.

I have held my grudge and rage against them long enough, I can't keep silent any longer. I know they are the cause of all my health issues, from the pinched nerve in my spine that causes my legs to lock up to my Strep arthritis that is caused from not being treated on time for strep throat because they thought I was "faking" my illnesses. Well, who is lying now?

I know many of you will ridicule them after reading this and I say to you have at it, ruin their lives like they ruined mine, all I have to say karma bites hard.

My trauma still sticks with me to this day, I have tried a therapy, but that isn't helpful. My anxiety triggers and can lead to seizures now, especially if I am over stressed. I am overprotective of my children and family because I never had that level of protection from when I was a child. As a result of no food being available when I would visit my mom in Nebraska's home and my parents, my body hasn't been able to gain weight and because of all the junk food that was available to eat rather than healthy food, my body can no longer eat sugary foods or other junk foods, so I am on a kidney friendly diet. I explain in my book *The Kidney Friendly Diet* on how I have gotten to the point I am at now.

If only things were different instead of discouraging me on what I want to do rather than telling me what is not even in my ability to do such as college because of my learning disability and as well as being a computer programmer for me is difficult because I don't understand math.

I am unable to drive because each time my dad tried to teach me or anyone else in my family would yell and scream at me, leading me to anxiety attacks, in fact to this day if I try and learn I get an anxiety attack when I sit behind the wheel of a car. As well, I am a bit concerned and so is my wife about my seizures too. That is the second reason why I don't drive a car.

I have tried to escape my past, but my past keeps coming back and haunt me. I feel like I have a metaphorical chain around my neck that cannot be broken because of the level of anger and stress that my parents have instilled in me because they hate themselves. There are times that I feel like I am being a bad father because for years my stepmom kept throwing in my face that I will be a terrible father because I can't ride a bike or like riding roller coasters, they even said I would be a bad husband and boyfriend because I have a fear of heights and fast rides. My parents have used words like that since I was little to try and ruin my self-esteem. It has worked for the most part to the point I second guess myself a lot, I question my wife if I am a good father or ask her if I am "boring" like my stepmom kept telling me for years.

I will never tear my children apart like they did to me, I don't care if they don't want to ride a bike or want to ride a roller coaster. All I care about is that they are safe and alive. They need to learn to respect the earth we live on. I don't mind them being on games. My children's safety is important to me. When my two-year-old daughter is old enough to ask questions, she will not be against me for not wanting to ride a roller coaster, my two stepchildren have no interest in places like that, and I am not against their wishes. My parents have been doing wrong, no parent should ever use psychological pain like that against any child.

I know my wife accepts me for my flaws, I accept her for hers, and my stepchildren as well, even my two-year-old will develop her own flaws when she gets older. I will not say to them that they won't make good "parents or spouses". That would be evil and cruel of me. Much like my parents have done to me. I will not be like my parents. I am more loving and caring than they are. If any of my children need help when they are adults, I will help them equally not help two of them and neglect the other like my parents have done to me.

Writing is what I know with all my heart and soul. It is my passion, without Authors, who could learn great works such as *Stephen king* or *Jane Roberts the Seth Materials*?